A Very Firm Handshake
- Confessions of a Charity Chief Executive

Ted Hill MBE

Copyright © 2024 by Ted Hill

ISBN: 978-1-917425-05-6

Preface

I worked in the voluntary sector for over 40 years, mostly at senior levels as CEO and during those 40 years I made many errors. The following stories cover a few of those, not all in the same organisation and I have changed names to protect the guilty.

I have used some poetic license with some of the stories, but most are very true, I will allow the reader to decide which is which.

There are some stories I have left out including, the two elderly trustees who nearly came to fisty cuffs over the location of a regional Christmas Party, the Luddite Chairman who refused to use email and insisted on only using the telephone & hand written letters, and the strange accusation that I was employing my illegitimate children in the organisation.

It would seem one such child was the result of a night of passion in Cardiff while I was in the navy. For the record I don't have any illegitimate children (that I know of) and I was a Sea Cadet Officer (RNR), not a scurrilous seafarer.

There are of course the stories I can never tell!

My thanks to my good friend Jon Gardner for his apt title suggestion and his memories of some of the incidents included in this book. My thanks also to another good friend, Ron Hughes for the cover design.

I have met hundreds of very committed worthy inspiring individuals over 40 years in the sector and a few less likable people as well, picked up the MBE along the way and it was a great career. I am now happily retired and volunteer with a local disability organisation, *Wetwheels Hamble* on the south coast of England where I am the Chair.

Chapter 1: Handshakes and Hijinks

- The story origin of the firm handshake: how a humble greeting became my superpower.
- The day I accidentally crushed a donor's hand (and still got the donation).
- Misadventures in etiquette: the elbow bump era.

Chapter 2: The Boardroom Circus

- Juggling acts: balancing egos, budgets, and a thousand opinions.
- The great coffee debacle: why we no longer serve decaf at meetings.
- How I convinced the board to approve a "puppy therapy" program.

Chapter 3: Gala Glitches

- Beam Me Up Scotty -.The Documentary Launch
- Dress codes and disasters: when black-tie meets The Boominator.
- Speech snafus: that time I thanked the wrong person… twice.

Chapter 4: Volunteer Vignettes & Staff Stories

- The Dress
- Squid Squid!
- Surviving the Bake Sale
- Spontaneous Combustion of Raffle tickets
- Universal Entry
- The Musical Interviewee
- The Shy Interviewee
- Hats Off to Ascot
- Not Everyone is Nice

Chapter 5: Donor Dynamics
- The art of the thank-you note: how a typo almost cost us a fortune.
- The mysterious benefactor: Too Good to be True.
- How to say no politely when offered a second-hand yacht.

Chapter 6: Office Antics
- The legendary office move prank war.
- What a Mug
- Open plan problems: the saga of the communal fridge.

Chapter 7: Social Media Shenanigans
- The tweet that went viral for all the wrong reasons.
- Meme magic: using humor to boost donations.

Chapter 8: International Incidents
- Lost in translation: when our slogan meant something entirely different overseas.
- The day I learned what "business casual" means in different countries.

Chapter 9: The Lighter Side of Legalities
- Navigating the labyrinth of charity law with a sense of humor.
- Paperwork Overload.
- Board Meeting Bingo
- The Oops Clause
- Audit Antics
- Trademark Tremors

Chapter 1:
Handshakes and Hijinks

The Origin Story of the Firm Handshake: How a Humble Greeting Became My Superpower

The Day I Accidentally Crushed a Donor's Hand (and Still Got the Donation)

My journey to becoming a Charity Chief Executive wasn't marked by Oxbridge degrees or a string of prestigious internships. No, my rise to the top began with something far simpler and, perhaps, more powerful: a handshake. Not just any handshake, mind you, but a very firm handshake.

My good friend Jon said, "Ted a good way to make a quick good first impression is a Very Firm Handshake", I took him at his word.

It was a sunny Tuesday in a usually rainy North Finchley, the kind of day where the birds seem to be in perfect harmony and the sky is that particular shade of blue that makes everything feel possible. Our charity was hosting a lunch to thank our top donors and I was especially excited to meet Mr. Thomas, a potential major benefactor whose generous contributions could significantly bolster our community outreach programs.

Mr. Thomas was an older gentleman with a reputation for being both immensely wealthy and notoriously difficult to impress. Rumor had it that he once turned down a pitch simply because he didn't like the font used in the presentation materials. I knew that meeting him would be a make-or-break moment for our organisation.

As I walked into the ornate old library, I spotted Mr. Thomas standing near the buffet table, scrutinising a particularly rebellious crab cake. Summoning my confidence, I approached him with my best professional smile. "Mr. Thomas, a pleasure to finally meet you. My name is Ted and I'm the Chief Executive of the charity."

He turned slowly, his eyes meeting mine with an expression that could curdle milk. Undeterred, I extended my hand, ready to deliver my signature firm handshake. As our hands clasped, I applied the usual pressure, but something went terribly wrong. Mr. Thomas's face contorted into a grimace, and I realised with horror that my handshake was far too firm.

There was a distinct crack. I had crushed his hand.

Time seemed to freeze as Mr. Thomas let out a small, dignified yelp. The room fell silent, and all eyes were on us. Panic surged through me. In that split second, my entire career flashed before my eyes, each failed attempt at impressing this crucial donor piling up in my mind like a stack of rejected grant applications.

"Oh my goodness, Mr. Thomas, I am so terribly sorry," I stammered, releasing his hand as if it were a live grenade. "I didn't mean to—are you alright?"

He looked at his hand, then at me, his eyes narrowing. The entire room held its breath, waiting for his verdict. Finally, he spoke, his voice surprisingly calm given the circumstances. "Young man," he said, (and I was a young man at the time) "that was quite the handshake. I haven't felt a grip like that since my days in the military."

I blinked, not sure if I was about to be complimented or escorted out by security.

"You remind me of my old drill sergeant," he continued, flexing his fingers gingerly. "Strong handshake, no nonsense. I like that."

I could barely believe what I was hearing. "Th-thank you, sir. Again, I apologise for the, uh, intensity."

He chuckled, a deep, rumbling sound that seemed to fill the entire room. "No need to apologise. It's good to see someone with some spirit and conviction. Too many people these days have the handshake of a wet fart."

Relief flooded through me, and I managed a nervous laugh. "Well, I certainly believe in a firm grip."

Mr. Thomas nodded thoughtfully. "Indeed. Now, tell me more about your charity. I like people who don't do things halfway."

Over the next hour, we talked in depth about our mission, our projects, and our vision for the future. Despite the shaky start, Mr. Thomas seemed genuinely impressed with our work and my earnest passion. By the end of our conversation, he had not only forgiven my overly enthusiastic handshake but had also pledged a significant donation to our cause.

As he was leaving, he turned to me and said, "Remember, young man, a firm handshake can open many doors. Just be careful not to break too many hands along the way."

From that day forward, I made sure to moderate my handshake technique, adjusting the pressure according to the recipient. But the story of how I accidentally crushed Mr. Thomas's hand and still secured his donation became a legendary tale in our organisation, a testament to the strange and wonderful power of a very firm handshake.

Misadventures in Etiquette: The Elbow Bump Era

If there's one thing the Covid global pandemic taught us, it's how to adapt to new norms with varying degrees of success. Gone were the days of firm handshakes and cheeky high-fives. Enter the era of the Namaste and the less elegant elbow bump, a gesture that quickly became the gold standard for pandemic-safe greetings. As the Chief Executive of a charity, I knew embracing this new etiquette was essential, but little did I know how challenging—and downright comical—it would be.

Our first major event post-lockdown was the annual general meeting, the annual death by power point with few attendees. This year though people wanted an excuse to get out and we reimagined our AGM as a hybrid affair with both in-person and virtual elements. To comply with health guidelines, we decided to adopt the elbow bump as the official greeting of the evening. My team and I practiced diligently, ensuring we had the perfect technique: a quick, confident bump, just high enough to be polite but not too forceful. We were ready!

The day of the AGM arrived, and the hall was abuzz with excitement. As guests trickled in, I stood at the entrance, ready to welcome them with my newly mastered elbow bump. The first few greetings went smoothly, with just the right mix of enthusiasm and restraint. But then, things started to unravel.

My first notable mishap occurred with Mrs. Jones, a sweet elderly lady who had been a long-time supporter of our charity. As she approached, I extended my elbow with a bright smile. Unfortunately, Mrs. Jones, who wasn't quite as up-to-date on the latest greeting trends, leaned in for a traditional cheek kiss at the exact same moment. The result was a rather awkward and unexpected collision, leaving us both blushing and stammering apologies.

Next came Mr. Dale, a tall, burly man (I am a good 5'6 in my socks) whose idea of an elbow bump resembled more of a rugby tackle. As our elbows met, the force of his enthusiasm nearly sent me stumbling backwards into the coat rack. "Sorry, old chap! Got a bit carried away!" he boomed, while I tried to regain my composure and prevent the rack from collapsing entirely.

Then there was the case of young Timmy, the precocious son of one of our major members. Timmy, clearly more accustomed to fist bumps, interpreted my extended elbow as an invitation for a playful punch. His tiny fist made contact with surprising accuracy, and I had to bite back a yelp while maintaining a gracious smile. "Nice to see you too, Timmy," I managed through gritted teeth.

As the event progressed, the elbow bumps became increasingly unpredictable. One guest mistook my gesture for a mime performance and tried to "mirror" my movements, resulting in a bizarre dance routine that left us both looking like we were auditioning for Strictly or worse a slapstick comedy. Another, attempting to be overly cautious, missed my elbow entirely and ended up jabbing me in the ribs.

Despite these misadventures, the AGM was a resounding success. We all enjoyed meeting people face to face and the virtual attendees raved about the innovative format. As the event ended, I reflected on the AGM with a mixture of amusement and exhaustion.

The next morning, my inbox was flooded with messages from guests, many of whom shared their own hilarious elbow bump stories. It seemed that our attempts at pandemic etiquette had provided much-needed comic relief in an otherwise challenging time. One particularly memorable email came from Mr. Dale, who wrote, "Thanks for the great evening! My wife says I should tone down my elbow bumps. Hope your ribs are okay!"

The elbow bump era may have been short-lived, but it left a lasting impression. It reminded us that, even during unprecedented circumstances, the spirit of human connection could prevail, albeit in unexpected ways. And as for me, I learned to approach new trends with a healthy dose of humor and flexibility—lessons that have served me well in navigating the ever-evolving landscape of charity work.

So, while the firm handshake remains my superpower, I now keep an elbow bump in my arsenal, ready for those moments when adaptability and a good laugh are just what the occasion calls for.

Chapter 2:
The Boardroom Circus

Juggling Acts: Balancing Egos, Budgets, and a Thousand Opinions

Being the Chief Executive of a charity is often akin to performing in a three-ring circus, and I, apparently, was the ringmaster. Little did I know that managing a nonprofit would require not only a firm handshake but also the balancing skills of a seasoned juggler. The three primary juggling balls? Egos, budgets, and a thousand opinions.

Egos

One particular Trustee board meetings were "interesting". Meetings were a spectacle in themselves. Imagine a room filled with accomplished and some less accomplished individuals, each with their own vision of how the charity should be run. There was Mrs. Manners, our seasoned treasurer, who took immense pride in her decades of financial stewardship. Then there was Mr. Flynn, the young tech-savvy marketing guru, whose ideas often clashed with Mrs. Manners more traditional approach. And let's not forget Mr. Litten, the passionate advocate for our mission, whose speeches could rival those of a seasoned politician, especially if it involved Scotland.

Navigating these personalities required diplomacy and the occasional use of creative flattery. "Mrs. Manners, your meticulous budgeting has been the backbone of our financial stability," I'd start, watching her preen slightly. "And Mr. Broen, your innovative ideas are exactly what we need to attract a younger demographic." This balancing act was a delicate dance of acknowledging each person's contributions while gently steering them towards a common goal.

One memorable incident involved the infamous "office plant" debate. Mrs. Manners was adamant that a large portion of the budget should go towards new accounting software, while Mr. Broen was equally passionate about creating an indoor green space to boost staff morale in our new building. The meeting grew tense, with raised voices and pointed fingers. Just as I feared a full-blown mutiny, I proposed a compromise: a smaller budget for plants and a trial run of the software. They grudgingly agreed, and I managed to avoid a horticultural civil war.

Budgets

Ah, budgets—**the bane of every** Chief Executive's existence. Crafting a budget that satisfies everyone's needs while ensuring the charity's sustainability is like trying to bake a cake with too few ingredients and too many cooks in the kitchen.

Our annual budgeting meetings were a spectacle to behold. Mrs. Manners would present a meticulously detailed spreadsheet of several pages, her eyes sparkling with the thrill of numerical precision. Meanwhile, our program directors would each present their wish lists, ranging from new community outreach programs to advanced training for our volunteers.

Balancing these demands was no small feat. I remember one year when we faced a particularly tight budget. We had just lost a major grant, and tough decisions had to be made. I spent sleepless nights pouring over numbers, cutting costs here, reallocating funds there. When I finally presented the revised budget, the room was silent. I braced myself for the backlash.

To my surprise, Mrs. Manners spoke first. "I appreciate the effort to maintain our financial health," she said, and the tension in the room eased. It wasn't perfect, but it was a start. The Trustees grumbled but accepted the cuts, and we moved forward. It was in moments like these that I learned the art of compromise and the importance of transparent communication.

A Thousand Opinions

If balancing egos and budgets wasn't enough, there were always a thousand opinions to consider. From staff members, to volunteers, to the community we served; everyone had a perspective on how things should be done. And let's not forget the donors & funders, whose feedback often came with the unspoken addendum, **"Or else."**

One particularly chaotic episode involved our rebranding efforts. Our logo, a relic from the 1960s, desperately needed an update. We formed a committee, conducted surveys, and came up with a design. Simple enough, right? Wrong. The new logo was revealed, and the floodgates opened.

"I miss the old logo; it had character," lamented a long-time volunteer.

"The new design doesn't reflect our mission," opined Mr Atkins.

"I think it's too modern," sniffed Mrs. Manners.

Caught in the crossfire, I organised a town hall meeting to gather feedback and discuss the rationale behind the new design. It was a tense affair, with strong opinions on all sides. But by the end, we reached a consensus: a few tweaks here, a color change there, and we had a logo that everyone could live with, if not love. The process taught me that while you can't please everyone, you can create a sense of inclusion and shared purpose.

We entered our efforts for the Third Sector Awards and got shortlisted – so not too shabby!

The Balancing Act

Balancing egos, budgets, and a thousand opinions is an ongoing juggling act, one that requires patience, resilience, and a sense of humor. I've learned to embrace the chaos, to find joy in the small victories, and to never underestimate the power of a well-timed compliment.

In the end, it's the passion and dedication of everyone involved that keeps the charity moving forward. And I knew as long as I could keep the balls in the air—without too many hitting the ground— we would continue to make a difference, one carefully balanced step at a time.

The Great Coffee Debacle: Why We No Longer Serve Decaf at Meetings

In the world of charity leadership, meetings are the lifeblood of decision-making. They're where strategies are formed, budgets are approved, and egos are, hopefully, managed. And what fuels these critical gatherings? Coffee. Strong, black, caffeinated coffee. Yet, there was a time when we naively believed that offering a variety of coffee options, including decaf, would cater to everyone's tastes. This, dear reader, was a grave mistake.

It all started innocently enough. Our office manager suggested we diversify our coffee offerings. "Not everyone wants the jitters," she reasoned. "Some people prefer decaf." Being a forward-thinking leader, I agreed. After all, how much trouble could a pot of decaf cause?

We introduced decaf at the next board meeting, placing two shiny carafes on the table: one labeled "Regular" and the other "Decaf." I thought nothing of it as I made my way to the head of the table, ready to dive into our agenda.

The first sign of trouble came about 15 minutes in, when Mrs. Manners, our meticulous treasurer, began tapping her pen at an increasing speed. Normally calm and composed, she seemed unusually agitated. "Where are the budget projections for the next quarter?" she snapped, her eyes narrowing at me over her glasses.

Mr. Boen, our young marketing whiz, wasn't faring any better. He fidgeted in his seat, his usual enthusiasm replaced by a jittery impatience. "Can we speed this up? I have a campaign launch to oversee."

Meanwhile, Mr Long, who typically delivered impassioned but measured speeches about our mission, was uncharacteristically quiet, staring blankly at his notes as if they were written in ancient Greek.

I began to sense that something was amiss. A tension filled the room, thick and palpable. It wasn't until the Office Manager leaned over and whispered, "I think there's been a mix-up with the coffee," that the pieces of the puzzle fell into place.

"Are you saying…?" I trailed off, my eyes widening.

She nodded. "I think the decaf and regular got switched."

My mind raced. The Regular coffee pot, which we had assumed was fueling our decision-making, was in fact decaf. And the Decaf pot? Pure, unadulterated caffeine, coursing through the veins of those who specifically sought to avoid it.

I glanced around the table. Mrs. Manners was now furiously scribbling numbers, muttering about fiscal responsibility. Mr. Flynns's leg bounced up and down at a speed that suggested he might take off into the air at any moment while Mr Boen seemed on the verge of a nap.

"Ladies and gentlemen," I said, raising my hands in a bid for calm. "It appears there has been a slight coffee mix-up. If you're feeling a bit… off, you might have had the wrong brew."

There was a collective pause as everyone processed this revelation. Then, chaos.

"I knew something was wrong!" Mrs. Manners exclaimed, her tapping pen clattering to the table.

"No wonder I feel like I'm running on fumes," grumbled Mr. Flynn.

Mr. Boen simply sighed, reaching for yet another cup of what he hoped was the real deal this time.

We took a short break to sort out the coffee debacle. The Office Manager hastily relabeled the carafes, and we all took a moment to reset. The meeting resumed, but the damage was done. Discussions were fraught with lingering irritation and fatigue.

The aftermath of the Great Coffee Debacle led to a unanimous decision: no more decaf. Our board members needed to be alert, focused, and at their best, and the risk of another mix-up was too great. From that day forward, only the strongest, most caffeinated coffee graced our meetings, or water.

In the grand scheme of things, the debacle became a legendary cautionary tale within our organisation, a reminder of how small details can derail even the best-laid plans. It also taught me the importance of adaptability and humor in leadership. After all, if you can't laugh at a room full of caffeine-deprived board members, what can you laugh at?

And so, armed with the right coffee, we continue to face the challenges of charity work, one highly caffeinated meeting at a time.

As an aside my other half, Maggie has terrible withdrawal effects if she doesn't get her tea and believe me nobody wants to see that!

How I Convinced the Board to Approve a "Puppy Therapy" Program

While working in mental health, convincing a board of seasoned professionals to approve a "puppy therapy" program for our charity was not only one of my proudest achievements but also one of the most fun and heartwarming experiences of my career. The idea of bringing in dogs to provide therapeutic benefits to our clients seemed, to me, like a no-brainer. However, getting the board on board (pun intended) required a mix of strategy, charm, and a bit of puppy magic.

The idea sprouted during a particularly challenging period for our organisation. Our clients, all in residential mental health care were facing increased stress and anxiety due to the tumultuous social and economic climate, and our staff was equally strained. We needed a fresh, innovative approach to boost morale and provide emotional support.

I first encountered the concept of puppy therapy at a wellness conference, where a group of adorable puppies was brought in to help attendees unwind. The sight of business professionals, usually so serious and stoic, melting into puddles of joy as they played with the pups was unforgettable. The experience sparked a thought: if it could work for stressed executives, it could certainly work for our clients and staff.

Armed with research and a vision, I prepared to pitch the idea at our next board meeting. But I knew this wouldn't be easy. Our board was composed of individuals with diverse backgrounds, including finance, healthcare, and community service. They were pragmatic, budget-conscious, and sometimes resistant to what they might perceive as frivolous ideas.

I began by gathering solid evidence to support the benefits of puppy therapy. Studies showed that interaction with animals could reduce stress, lower blood pressure, and improve overall mental well-being. I compiled case studies from other organisations that had successfully implemented similar programs and highlighted their positive outcomes.

I also reached out to local animal shelters and therapy dog organisations to understand the logistics and costs involved. This groundwork was crucial in addressing any practical concerns the board might have.

I crafted my pitch with a balance of emotional appeal and hard data. I knew the key was to connect the idea to our charity's mission and demonstrate how it aligned with our goals of improving the lives of those we served.

"Imagine," I began, "a room filled with laughter and joy as our clients, many of whom face daily struggles, find comfort and companionship with a furry friend. Picture our staff, recharged and rejuvenated, ready to tackle their demanding tasks with renewed energy and positivity. Puppy therapy is not just about cute animals; it's about fostering a supportive, healing environment."

On the day of the meeting, I brought in a surprise guest: Max, a golden retriever puppy from a local therapy dog organisation. As the board members filed into the room, Max greeted them with wagging tail and soulful eyes. The atmosphere immediately lightened, and I saw smiles spread across even the sternest faces.

I began my presentation with a slideshow of statistics and testimonials, but it was Max who truly stole the show. I highlighted the minimal costs, which could be offset by partnering with local shelters and applying for wellness grants. I also pointed out the potential for positive publicity, which could attract new donors and volunteers.

When I finished, I could see the board members were intrigued but still needed convincing. That's when I played my ace card: a video montage of clients from a similar program, their faces glowing with happiness as they interacted with the puppies. There wasn't a dry eye in the room.

The board raised practical questions about allergies, safety, and logistics. I was prepared. I explained that we would ensure a controlled environment, with thorough health and safety protocols. We would offer the program on an opt-in basis, ensuring that no one with allergies or aversions would be forced to participate.

The final vote came down to a blend of pragmatism and passion. Mr Small, ever the budget hawk, admitted that the cost was reasonable given the potential benefits. Mr. Khan, the marketing guru, pointed out the positive PR and community engagement opportunities. Mr. Norman, whose heart always lay with our clients, was visibly moved by the emotional impact.

When the votes were tallied, the puppy therapy program was approved unanimously. The room erupted in applause, and Max celebrated by rolling over for belly rubs.

The implementation of the puppy therapy program had a bit of a false start. One of our senior managers said she would be happy to bring in her two puppies, and she did. What she failed to say though was that these puppies were in fact quite large Alsatians who preferred to walk up and down the veranda as if on guard.

"Looks like a prison" as one client put it, and she was right, it looked like the set of Stalag Luft 3 in *The Great Escape*.

We moved on and the programme exceeded all expectations. Our clients eagerly anticipated their "puppy days," and the staff morale soared. The sight of clients and staff bonding with the puppies became a cherished part of our organisation's culture.

Convincing the board to approve the puppy therapy program was a testament to the power of a well-crafted pitch, solid research, and a bit of adorable persuasion. It reminded us all that sometimes, the best solutions come with wagging tails and wet noses.

Chapter 3:
Gala Glitches

Beam me up Scotty!   The documentary launch
Charity galas & launches are often seen as the pinnacle of sophistication and elegance—an opportunity to dress up, mingle with influential donors, and celebrate the achievements of the organisation. But as anyone in the nonprofit world knows, even the best-laid plans can go hilariously, if not disastrously, awry. One such evening, which has since become the stuff of legend, was the night we launched our documentary.

The event, held at a prestigious London teaching hospital, was meant to be an unforgettable night. And unforgettable it was—but not for the reasons we had hoped. The preparations had been meticulous: gourmet catering, a live band, an auction with good prizes and meticulously arranged decor that transformed the rather dull room into a wonderland of twinkling fairy lights and lush floral arrangements.

But first, the documentary launch in the hospital's very own cinema!

The evening began without a hitch. Guests arrived in droves, dressed to the nines and ready to open their wallets for a good cause. Our international guest arrived. The band played smooth background music, the champagne flowed, and laughter echoed through the grand halls. I was in high spirits, making rounds and greeting our esteemed guests.

I walked on stage, and announced we were proud to launch our new documentary directed by a well-known international movie maker. I left the stage to applause ringing in my ears. The lights went down, the screen lit up and then ---- Oh My God. Rather than the documentary I had seen earlier in the run through in the office we got the film rushes. Bits and bobs of odd filming, bizarre cuts, out-takes and clips including a shot of one of the contributors talking about her red shoes. It was a bloody nightmare which still wakes me up.

For a moment, there was stunned silence, followed by the inevitable gasps and murmurs of confusion. After a few minutes and the realisation it was not going to get any better the Chair got onto the stage and apologised for the obvious error while I went to hunt down the Director, who had taken to his toes and was gone, never to be seen by us again.

Just to add to the nightmare, the international guest on leaving the cinema fell out of his wheelchair. Clearly help was immediate and full, the event being in a hospital and after a quick check over in A&E all was well. We have since become good friends, but I will never forget that night.

Dress Codes and Disasters: When Black-Tie Meets *The Boominator*

When organising a charity event, one of the first things to decide is the dress code. A black-tie event conveys elegance and sophistication, and it often encourages guests to open their wallets a little wider. But what happens when one guest's interpretation of black tie differs wildly from everyone else's? Allow me to recount the infamous time when our black-tie event met *The Boominator.*

We worked hard and moved into a new building. To reflect the enormity of the occasion we had an official opening by a royal dignitary accompanied by the great and the good. The invitations, printed on thick, creamy paper with gold foil accents, clearly stated the dress code: black-tie and encouraged medals to be worn- yes it was that kind of event.

The preparations were flawless. The new meeting space was perfect, tables were adorned with white linens and floral centerpieces, and classical music set the mood. I stood at the entrance, greeting guests as they arrived, each one more elegantly dressed than the last. Our Royal guest came accompanied by the Lord Lieutenant, MP, local Councilors etc and we officially opened the new offices. Fortunately, as luck would have it, the Royal dignitary had to leave for another engagement leaving those behind to mingle, say "what wonderful event" and listen to the speeches.

Everything was going perfectly until he walked in.

Boom! In came *The Boominator,* aka Heavy D or Colin Newell. Sadly Colin died in 2020 but at the time he was a heavy weight (in more ways than one) TV personality featuring on the TV programme Storage Hunters UK & Celebrity Big Brother.

He strutted into the room wearing the loudest, flamboyant, brightest "living it large" suit you can imagine. The room fell silent as heads turned and jaws dropped. The black-tie uniformity was abruptly shattered by *The Boominators* unique interpretation of formal attire. He was either blissfully unaware or perfectly content with his fashion choice as he loudly greeted fellow guests with a wide grin and hearty handshakes, during the Chairs speech.

To this day I do not know who invited him, how he got in past security nor indeed why he was there in the first place, but he was.

My first instinct was to panic. How would the other guests react? Would they be offended? But I quickly reminded myself that, above all, our events were about inclusivity and appreciation for our supporters, no matter how they dressed.

I approached *The Boominator* with a warm smile. "Mr. Newell, it's wonderful to see you. You certainly know how to make an entrance!"

He laughed heartily. "You know me, I like to stand out! And this suit? Custom made. Cost more than a tux!"

I chuckled along with him, appreciating his good humor and trying to diffuse any tension his outfit might have caused as I slowly dragged him away from the main event.

Instead of trying to downplay the situation, I decided to embrace it. "Ladies and gentlemen," I announced, drawing everyone's attention in one of the breaks, "let's all give a round of applause to *The Boominator* for bringing his unique flair to our opening!"

There was a hesitant pause as clearly most of our guests had no idea who he was. Colin stayed for about 20 minutes, ate a few sandwiches and was off as quickly as he arrived. The atmosphere lightened, and conversations resumed, with guests smiling and whispering about the unexpected turn of events, especially the Chair.

As the day progressed, I noticed something remarkable. *The Boominator* had became the unofficial star of the day. He was everything the event was not. His presence, initially a potential disaster, turned into a conversation starter and even helped some guests relax and enjoy the event more.

After the event, I received numerous messages from attendees praising the day. Surprisingly, many mentioned The Boominators arrival and outfit as a highlight, noting how it added a memorable and personal touch to the day. It was a reminder that while traditions and dress codes have their place, the heart of our events lies in the people who support our cause.

The incident of the **"Very Loud Suit"** taught me an invaluable lesson about flexibility and the importance of embracing diversity in all its forms, even in dress codes. It highlighted that our donors and supporters come from all walks of life and express their support in different ways. By welcoming these differences, we strengthen our community and our cause.

And so, while I would still encourage a black-tie dress code for those type of events, I do so with a touch of humor and an open heart, ready to welcome the unexpected and celebrate the individuality of all our guests. Because at the end of the day, it's not about the clothes we wear, but the hearts we bring to the table.

Speech Snafus: That Time I Thanked the Wrong Person... Twice

Public speaking is a critical skill for any charity executive, especially when it comes to delivering speeches at major events. These speeches are opportunities to inspire, to thank our supporters, and to rally everyone around our cause. However, even the best-prepared speeches can go awry, and I learned this the hard way when I managed to thank the wrong person not once, but twice, in front of a packed room.

The Volunteer Day event was off to a stellar start. The room was filled with our most generous donors, volunteers, and key stakeholders, all dressed to the nines and ready to celebrate our achievements. The mood was festive, the decorations were stunning, and the atmosphere buzzed with excitement. My task for the evening was to deliver a speech that not only highlighted our successes but also acknowledged the incredible contributions of specific individuals who had gone above and beyond in their support.

As the evening progressed, I felt a mix of nerves and excitement building. I had meticulously prepared my speech, making sure to include heartfelt thanks to several key donors. Among them were Mr. Anderson, a long-time benefactor whose substantial contributions had funded several of our major projects, and Ms. Smith, a passionate advocate whose volunteer efforts had made a significant impact.

I took the stage, feeling confident and energised. The spotlight was on me, and the room fell silent in anticipation. I began my speech, recounting the year's achievements and the challenges we had overcome. The audience responded warmly, and I felt a surge of pride and connection with everyone in the room.

Then came the moment to acknowledge our key supporters. "I'd like to extend a special thank you to Mr. Anderson for his incredible generosity and unwavering support," I announced, gesturing towards a man seated at a prominent table near the front.

Except, the man I gestured to wasn't Mr. Anderson. It was Mr. Harris, another donor, but not the one I intended to thank at that moment. Mr. Harris looked momentarily confused but smiled and nodded graciously. I caught the mistake almost immediately but decided to press on, hoping to correct it subtly later.

I continued with my speech, trying to regain my composure. "And of course, a heartfelt thanks to Ms. Smith, whose dedication and hard work have been invaluable to us," I said, looking towards where I believed Ms. Smith was seated.

This time, I gestured towards Ms. Toms, another committed volunteer, but again, not the right person. Ms. Toms gave a polite smile, clearly puzzled by the unexpected recognition.

By now, a few people in the audience were starting to exchange glances, and I could feel the heat rising on my cheeks. Determined to set things right, I decided to correct my errors directly. "I apologise, I seem to have been mixed up in my excitement. Thank you, Mr. Anderson," I said, pointing this time towards the real Mr. Anderson.

Only, to my horror, I had pointed at yet another wrong person—Mr. Jenkins, who had graciously sponsored the evening's dinner. Mr. Anderson, seated two tables away, raised his hand slightly, trying to help me out, but the damage was done. The room, now a mix of polite chuckles and sympathetic smiles, was fully aware of my blunders.

Realising that the only way out was to embrace the situation with humor, I took a deep breath and said, "Well, it seems that in my eagerness to thank everyone, I've managed to thank the wrong people several times. Let's get it right. Mr. Anderson, please stand up so we can all give you the proper applause you deserve."

Mr. Anderson stood, and the room erupted in applause. "And Ms. Smith, would you also stand and accept our gratitude?" I continued, this time correctly identifying Ms Smith, who rose to a round of cheers.

"And to everyone else I accidentally thanked, know that you are deeply appreciated as well. Clearly, I need to work on my aiming skills!" The audience laughed, the tension broke, and the rest of the speech went smoothly.

After the event, many guests approached me to commend my handling of the situation. Fortunately, everyone found the mix-up amusing and were pleased with the eventual recognition, the mistaken honorees, were gracious and supportive, understanding that these things happen.

The experience taught me several valuable lessons about public speaking and leadership. First, always double-check your facts and familiarise yourself with the key individuals you'll be acknowledging. Second, when mistakes happen—and they will—embrace them with humor and honesty. People appreciate authenticity and the ability to laugh at oneself. Finally, remember that the essence of these events is about connection and gratitude, and a few blunders can't overshadow the genuine appreciation behind the words.

In the end, the speech snafu became a memorable highlight of the evening, a reminder that even in our most polished moments, it's our imperfections that often bring us closer together.

Chapter 4:
Volunteer Vignettes & Staff Stories

The Dress

I am really not sure who came up with the original idea, but we decided we wanted to highlight the case of poor rail transport for people in wheelchairs. What better than to create a dress made from used railway tickets which one of our ambassadors could wear on a train - I know crazy, but that's how we rolled back then.

We had contact with a dress designer known for creating dresses from quirky material such as playing cards, crisp bags and plastic gloves so old rail tickets were right up her street. The dress was made and one of our ambassadors who uses a wheelchair agreed to wear it on a train ride from London to Scotland.

The first problem was that despite being booked the disability area on the train had been double booked – probably best highlighting the transport issue directly. So, the journey was cancelled, and we decided to take lots of photos outside the station and in a local park.

All going well, lots of attention and publicity. However, when we arrived at the park, we were met by Sergie, a photographer who just pitched up. Again, no idea how he found out or got there and he was a delight, if not a little strange speaking in a voice not dissimilar to Sergie of Meercat fame possibly explained by his very tight jeans.

One of the staff arranged for the dress to be transported back to the designer from London and ordered a box to be sent to the Premier Inn where our ambassador was staying for transport.

The phone rang and it was the Prem saying the box had arrived and could we collect it as soon as possible as it was taking up too much room in reception. My first reaction was to think the Prem was a little impatient but when we arrived to collect, I understood why they were anxious.

I think our staff member Susan had confused cm with meters and had ordered the biggest box in the world. It did take up most of reception, so they were quite right to raise the matter. I did suggest they could let out the box as another one of their rooms, but this fell on stoney ground and did not even get a titter from the manager who was looking close to losing it.

Squid Squid!

Out on the election trail when I was the Campaign Organiser for a north London constituency (a sort of political CEO) I was walking down a residential street with a Lord who had been a very popular MP in the same constituency in what is a ward with high Greek Cypriot roots.

A larger-than-life political character he stroud down the road shouting "Good Morning, Good Morning!" at the top of his voice in his best Greek. Sadly though, he was shouting "Calamari, Calamari!" instead of "Kalimera, Kalimera!".

A simple mistake but it raised interest from resident wanting to know why he was shouting "Squid Squid!"

Surviving the Annual Bake Sale

Organising a bake sale might sound like a straightforward endeavor—gather volunteers, bake some goodies, and sell them for a good cause. But as any seasoned charity chief executive knows, the annual bake sale can turn into a battlefield of flour, sugar, and unexpected challenges. Here's a glimpse into our adventures and misadventures with the beloved bake sale.

Months before the event, our team would gather to strategise. The bake sale was a staple fundraiser for our charity, drawing in families, local businesses, and sweet-toothed supporters alike. Volunteers were the heart and soul of our bake sale. We'd put out the call for bakers, and the response was always heartwarming. From grandmothers with secret cookie recipes to amateur bakers eager to display their skills, our kitchen brigade was as diverse as our community.

As the big day approached, the kitchen would transform into a whirlwind of activity. Batches of cookies, trays of brownies, and towers of cupcakes emerged from ovens in a symphony of tantalising aromas. Of course, not everything went according to plan. There were burnt batches, collapsed cakes, and the occasional culinary experiment gone awry (looking at you, avocado brownies).

On the morning of the sale in our temporary offices, we'd arrive early to set up tables adorned with colorful tablecloths and banners proudly displaying our charity's mission. Volunteers would arrange the treats with care, creating a mouthwatering display designed to entice even the most sugar-shy passerby.

Then came the rush. Local office workers on their lunch breaks, and curious neighbours would descend upon our bake sale like a hungry horde. The energy was infectious as volunteers manned the tables, making sales and sharing stories about the treats on offer.

Of course, not everything was smooth sailing. There were moments of chaos—sudden rainstorms threatening our outdoor setup, unexpected shortages of popular items, and the perennial challenge of keeping track of sales amidst the flurry of activity.

But through it all, there were moments of pure joy. The child whose eyes lit up at the sight of a rainbow cupcake, the elderly couple sharing a slice of homemade pie, the local

business owner who bought out an entire tray of cookies—
all reminded us of why we did what we did.

The annual bake sale taught us valuable lessons in teamwork, resilience, and the power of community spirit. It wasn't just about raising funds (though that was important)—it was about bringing people together, creating memories, and sharing a little sweetness in a sometimes-challenging world.

As we cleaned up the last crumbs and bid farewell to another successful bake sale, we knew that we'd be back next year, ready to tackle new challenges and create more tales from the trenches. Because when you're in the business of making a difference, every cookie sold, every smile shared, and every mishap survived is a story worth telling.

That said, it was not a piece of cake.

Spontaneous Combustion of Raffle Tickets

On a chilly December Wednesday, the office was bustling with excitement. The annual Christmas Raffle Draw was in full swing, with the scent of roasted chestnuts and the sound of Christmas music filling the air. The highlight of the day was always the grand raffle, with tickets sold throughout the month leading up to Christmas. This year, the prizes were especially enticing so had generated a lot of interest and ticket sales.

Arnold, a long-standing trustee of the Committee, paced anxiously near the raffle tub. The tub, a large popup bin had been decorated with holly and ribbons, was filled to the brim with thousands of brightly colored tickets. Arnolds's concern was etched on his face as he glanced at the tub every few minutes, his mind racing with worry.

"Arnold, are you alright?" asked Mary, another trustee, noticing his agitation.

Arnold sighed and rubbed his temples. "I'm just... uneasy, Mary. I've seen things go wrong before, and I can't shake the feeling that something could happen."

Mary frowned. "What do you mean? Everything seems to be in order."

Arnold took a deep breath and lowered his voice. "Years ago, at a similar event in another town, there was a fire. The raffle tickets, packed tightly together, spontaneously combusted. It happened so quickly—one moment everything was fine, the next, the tickets were ablaze. We were lucky no one got hurt, but the incident left a mark on me."

Mary's eyes widened in shock. "I had no idea. But what caused it?"

Arnold explained, "The tickets were stored in a container that didn't allow for proper ventilation. Combined with the dry paper and the friction from shuffling, it created the perfect conditions for combustion. I know it sounds far-fetched, but it happened."

Mary looked at the tub, then back at Arnold. "Maybe we should take some precautions, just in case. Can we ventilate the tub somehow?"

Arnold nodded. "That's exactly what I was thinking. If we make sure there's enough air circulation and keep an eye on the temperature, we should be able to prevent anything from going wrong."

They quickly set to work, carefully lifting the lid of the tub and creating small, unobtrusive holes around its sides to allow for airflow. Arnold instructed the volunteers to gently stir the tickets occasionally, ensuring they weren't packed too tightly. Arnold kept a vigilant watch, his heart easing slightly as time passed.

"Ladies and gentlemen, the winner of this year's grand raffle is... ticket number 4527!" The crowd erupted in cheers as a jubilant couple made their way to the stage to claim their prize.

Arnold allowed himself a smile, feeling a weight lift off his shoulders. Mary approached him, her eyes twinkling with gratitude. "You did it, Arnold. You kept everyone safe."

Arnold nodded; the relief evident in his voice. "I just couldn't bear the thought of something going wrong. Not again."

I just did'nt have the heart to tell him, raffle tickets don't spontaneously combust.

Universal Entry

Working with a Premier League football team for one charity two colleagues and I were invited to attend a match for an event. We were given our entry tickets to the stadium and behind the scenes access which was an old envelope with a hand written message on the back signed by the manager.

"*Entry for three*" it said. A bit surprised at the simplicity of it all, I was more surprised when we were waved through by security.

"He does this all the time" they said.

The Musical Interviewee

I was interviewing with one of my colleagues Bernard for an Admin Assistant post. Interviewees came & went all very capable, then in walked George. George had a good CV, good level of experience and seemed to have the key skills we were looking for. Asking the same question for the umpteenth time Bernard said: "So what are your keyboard skills like?"

George was quick to respond. "Well I can play a bit of piano but I am a bit rusty."

Not knowing how to react I tried to steer George in the direction of his experience with IT. At the same time

Bernards shoulders are visible bouncing up and down as he struggled to stifle the laugh of loud response the comment deserved and at the same time Bernard is kicking me under the table. We got through the rest of the interview. Just.

The Shy Interviewee

During the time of lockdown I was interviewing for a regional assistant. The job was to be the face of the charity locally and deal with local issues. Because of lockdown and as everyone was working from home a Zoom interview seemed the best way forward.

All was going well with surprisingly no difficulties with the IT but then Jane's appointment arrived. My colleague Georgina & I sat waiting for Jane to arrive so we could kick off the interview. There was a distant & hesitant voice from the laptop, "Hello?"

"Hello" I responded, "We can hear you Jane but we can't see you, can you turn your camera on?"

"No" was the quick response.

"Ok, is there a technical issue?

"No"

"OK, what the problem then?"

"I don't want people to see me, I am not comfortable with that"

"OK, but you do realise a main part of the job is representing the charity and when are we able going out to meet the community?

"I don't want to do that"

We carried on with the interview and scored appropriately. Still not sure why she actually applied.

Hats Off to Ascot

Picture the scene. A dozen or so striking hats – all with a sporting theme - being worn by models on Ladies' Day at Royal Ascot. The ladies wearing the hats were being 'papped' like nobody's business and French TV were even interviewing the guy who made it all possible.

Was this a promotional stunt by PRADA, Givenchy or Dolce & Gabbana? You might think so, but no, this was a small disability charity's creative idea to get a lesser-known condition and syndrome some airtime in the media, raise the charity's profile and perhaps improve the coffers to help support the charity and its cause.

A range of striking hats were on show including one to recognise Leicester City's Premier League triumph, a natty Saracens' rugby club hat, a Spurs' cockrell and 4 that depicted the national flags of England and Wales who would be playing each other in the Euros that day – among others.

Seeing the colourful, eye-catching hats on display at Ascot and seeing the models (staff) enthusiastically lap up the media attention was the tip of the iceberg and didn't tell the full story whowever.

Behind the scenes there had been already (and were further developing) a multitude of panics. An up-and-coming fashion designer had kindly agreed to make the hats for the charity for a peppercorn fee, on the basis that she would get some recognition, profile and hopefully some commissions. Bravo. A meeting had been held several months in advance to ascertain a) whether the designer was a real person b) whether they were up to the job and c) whether the brief was realistic in the timescales. All good.

Weekly turning into daily communications then ensued between the charity, the designer, the charity's PR agency and the various charity Ambassadors and staff who were going to be wearing the hats. One specific hat (you could call it the most important one) was being specially designed for an important charity Ambassador with a particular interest in a specific sport. The hat would be a show-stopper. The second most important hat (for another important charity Ambassador) needed to be spot on, too. Not to mention any problems with any hats during the numerous weekly/daily calls with the hat designer until a few hours (!) before the event. "I'm not 100% sure hats A, B and C are gonna be ready in time but I'll do my best".

"That could be a problem," I thought. The most important 2 hats did not materialise and I, the Marketing Manager and PR agency were left to pick up the pieces, placating disgruntled Ambassadors while trying to service the world's media who were seriously interested in some of the hats that had actually been produced – notably the England and Wales ones. Despite these not being 'The Best' hats on display, there was a lesson here that nothing gets in the way of a good story link. Linking the footy to Ascot Ladies' Day was a master stroke, even though we say so ourselves.

On the other hand what wasn't a master stroke, - I thought that you could just buy an expensive ticket for Royal Ascot, and rock up as a member of the public in a natty hat as I thought that was the entire purpose of Ladies' Day. Wrong. So apart from the ensuing dramas with hatless Ambassadors, there were also a number of models (charity employees) who were unable to get in to Ascot because the man with the *Jobsworth hat* had seen some Channel 4 tv footage and issued an edict to all gate staff: "Don't let in anyone wearing funny hats looking like the badges of sporting clubs." So, the gate people diligently followed the instruction and people were left outside frantically messaging: "What do we do now"?

So why were these charity hats initially banned from entry, even though all models had a valid ticket which the charity had paid handsomely for? "Too commercial," the word came back. OMG. Promoting a rare medical condition through creative hats – unbranded one might add – at a global event known for pushing the boundaries of ladies' fashion creativity… "too commercial."

Using all the tricks (experience) in the book, we managed to get all hat wearers into 'the building.' Nobody was arrested for paying to enter Royal Ascot while wearing a hat promoting a rare medical condition that few knew about. Blimey, how did we pull that off?

Best still, the campaign generated many millions of pounds worth of exposure in national and international media, predominantly featuring the England/Wales hats, and hundreds of thousands of clicks to a dedicated landing page set up for the day.

And why, I hear you say, did the most important hats not show up on the day, without warning? A little bird (canary) told us that the hat designer was maxing out on the opportunity and had agreed (with someone else) to showcase a new range of her own hats at Royal Ascot Ladies' Day for a major media launch – on the same day! How any of our hats got produced is an absolute miracle.

Further fantastic vignettes along the way on the day - apart from additional broadcast interviews with German TV, Channel 4 and the Racing Channel - included assistance with a charity photo shoot from a well-known racing tv pundit and a legendary national hunt jockey.

Further lessons learned from this highly successful/highly stressful event:

1) In Marketing & PR, as in life, the two often go together.

2) For all the best laid plans, things don't always go to plan.

3) You rarely have the full facts at your disposal – you're often lucky to get them all after the event.

4) Being agile and able to respond as situations unfold is really the strongest weapon to have in your locker,

5) Remember it's not ER, it's PR, as someone once said about the creative promotional industries; if your ideas are good and do you've done the best you can with the cards that have been dealt, then its job done. Try and enjoy these days and you can then relax with a well-earned beer at your leisure.

A final postscript to this equine episode is that it's often sometime after events and campaigns that their value is really known. And it's rarely the big numbers for media reach, advertising equivalent gained etc, that are the real deal for charities in particular, in the long-run.

The real benefit of all this noise at Ascot was that a potential (and very prominent) suitor to the charity saw the hats on Channel 4, picked up the phone to me, and it was the start of a long and fruitful commercial relationship for the charity.

And were the charity Trustees happy? No. Deep sigh!

Not Everyone is Nice
A ole1.
Quite recently I was involved in organising a Family Fun Day in the local community.

Everything had been organised to the last detail and to ensure no one parked on the carpark site the night before we had been out with very large No Parking signs, tape and cones as there would be an event the next day. It was obvious No Parking!

Arriving early the next morning to begin to set up there was, as predicted, a camper van parked bang in the middle of the car park. Clearly, he had arrived after we had left, ignored the signs, moved the cones/tape etc and parked up.

After 15 minutes or so the camper van doors opened, and a very rude and grumpy man got out to complain at the noise we were making.

"Sorry, you can't park here, there is a festival here today.," I declared, pointing to the brightly painted "No Parking" sign.

The now incensed campervan man pointed out he could park wherever he wanted, "This is a free country" his response littered with a few expletives and a lot of shouting and pointing.

I pointed out that the site was soon to be filled with stalls, classic cars, police vans, a fire engine and most of the local community. He would soon not be able to move out for the day. Again, undeterred, he disappeared into the camper, swearing and threatening all sorts of unmentionable things he would do to me.

I stood there thinking what to do, should I call the police for help as his behaviour might be threatening to the public or just build things up around him. After a few more minutes he reappeared, towel in hand walking at a pace to a marina shower block. I watched thinking should I say something more or just get on with it. He stopped abruptly, turned round and marched up to me. Was this going to be ugly? He stopped. "Sorry, but I need to park here". I then pointed out we had set up a temporary car park round the corner on a field at a price cheaper than that he would have paid at the car park.

A ole2

Volunteers worked at the temporary car park asking for a voluntary £5 to park, all proceeds to the charity and £5 being cheaper than the usual rate at the car park, now adorned with stalls gazebos and the like.

Radio messages came to the managing team of people parking without paying and simply ignoring the volunteers and stating they would be staying longer that the car park would be open. Volunteers politely pointed out there would be a significant release fee of £500 for late leavers, the fee imposed by the local council not us.

At closing time all the cars had gone.

Just goes to show though despite all the supportive people in the world there remain a few A -oles.

Chapter 5:
Donor Dynamics

The Art of the Thank-You Note: How a Typo Almost Cost Us a Fortune

In the realm of charity fundraising, the importance of expressing gratitude to donors cannot be overstated. A heartfelt thank-you note not only acknowledges their generosity but also strengthens the bond between the donor and the organisation. However, as I learned firsthand, even the most well-intentioned gestures can sometimes go hilariously, and alarmingly, awry.

It all began with a substantial donation from Mr. Dunn, a prominent local businessman known for his philanthropy. Mr. Dunn's donation was a game-changer for our charity, providing crucial funding for a new community outreach program we had been planning for months.

In the rush of excitement and gratitude, I hastily drafted a thank-you note to Mr. Dunn. The note was meant to convey our deepest appreciation for his generosity and the impact his donation would have on our initiatives. After carefully reviewing it—or so I thought—I hit send, confident that Mr. Dunn would be touched by our heartfelt message.

A few hours later, I received an urgent call from Mr. Dunn's assistant. "There seems to be a mistake in the thank-you note," she said, her tone a mix of concern and amusement.

My heart sank. I immediately pulled up the email to review what could have gone wrong. There, glaring back at me, was the offending typo: "Dear Mr. Dunn, thank you for your kind doantion…"

I was mortified. How could such a simple mistake slip through? I quickly composed a follow-up email to Mr.

Dunn, apologising profusely for the typo and assuring him that his donation was deeply valued and would be used effectively.

Mr. Dunn's response was gracious and understanding. He chuckled about the typo and assured me that he appreciated the sentiment regardless. However, he did gently remind me of the importance of attention to detail, especially in communications with donors.

The incident served as a valuable lesson for our team. We implemented stricter proofreading protocols for all donor communications, ensuring that every thank-you note was meticulously checked before sending. We also took the opportunity to personalise our interactions with donors further, recognising their individual contributions and the impact they were making.

As time passed, the typo incident became a humorous anecdote shared among staff and volunteers—a reminder of the pitfalls of rushing and the importance of thoroughness in our work. More importantly, it deepened our appreciation for the generosity of donors like Mr. Dunn and reinforced our commitment to maintaining strong relationships built on trust, respect, and attention to detail.

In the art of the thank-you note, every word matters. And while a typo may not have cost us a fortune in this case, it certainly taught us a priceless lesson in donor relations and the power of sincere gratitude.

The Mysterious Benefactor: If It's Too Good To Be True.....

In the world of charity fundraising, donors come in all shapes and sizes, each with their own motivations and stories. But every so often, there emerges a donor whose identity remains shrouded in mystery—a figure whose generosity speaks louder than words, yet whose anonymity adds an air of intrigue to their contributions. This is the tale of our own mysterious benefactor, whose legacy left a lasting impact on our organisation.

It all began one rainy afternoon when I received a call from one of our clinical advisors. One of his patients had asked if he could donate to our cause and who best to talk to. I was given the potential donors' contact details and phoned him to discuss expecting an offer of say £100 or so.

After talking to him for a while he said he wanted to fund research and I pointed out this was very expensive, but every penny counts. It was then he floored me with his offer of funding to the tune of several million pounds!

I checked I had heard correctly and yes, I had. This chap wanted to leave a legacy and we were it. I called the Chair and other key players, and it was agreed to pursue this further, which of course I did.

We held numerous meetings, planned how the funding would be spent and to be frank invested too much time and commitment

Sadly, the money that was expected from Trading deals, moving our cause to the next level, never materialised. The incident certainly reinforced a lifelong lesson, "If it's too good to be true – it probably is"

Declining an Offer of a Yacht

Politely declining an offer, especially one as generous as a second-hand yacht, requires tact and appreciation. I wanted to acknowledge the generosity of the offer, explain the decision clearly and respectfully, and ensure that the relationship with the offeror remained positive and appreciative.

I wrote a carefully worded letter stating that, after careful consideration, I had come to the difficult decision to decline the offer. While I was deeply honored by the kindness, I believed that maintaining a yacht would not align with current lifestyle and priorities.

Chapter 6:
Office Antics

The Legendary Office Move Prank War

In every workplace, there comes a time when the daily grind is punctuated by moments of laughter, camaraderie, and sometimes, a touch of mischief. One such occasion was the office move from a dodgy warehouse type environment to temporary offices before our big move to new purpose-built office space. This will forever be remembered as the year when our office transformed into the battleground for an epic prank war—an adventure that brought laughter, creativity, and unexpected camaraderie to the team.

It all started innocently enough, with a harmless prank pulled by Ron from Advocacy. He surreptitiously swapped out Karen's desk chair with an old squeaky one he found in storage. The resulting shrieks of surprise and laughter set the stage for what was to come.

Not to be outdone, Karen retaliated by covering Greg's desk in sticky notes while he was away at lunch. Every inch of his workspace—from computer monitor to stapler—was meticulously covered in neon-colored squares, creating a rainbow mosaic that greeted Ron upon his return.

From there, the prank war escalated with each participant upping the ante. Post-it notes evolved into plastic wrap covering entire cubicles. Desk drawers were filled with balloons. Fake spiders made surprising appearances in filing cabinets. Office supplies mysteriously disappeared, only to reappear in the communal kitchen with cryptic messages attached. Strange cups appeared in the kitchen with photos of former staff.

What started as a series of one-upmanship soon turned into a collaborative effort, with alliances forming and dissolving faster than a spilled coffee stain. Departments that rarely interacted found themselves conspiring late into the night, plotting the next elaborate prank to surprise their unsuspecting colleagues.

Susan even parceled herself up ready to be posted to the new office. Susan had a track record with boxes following the train ticket dress box incident.

Despite the chaos and occasional inconvenience (like the day someone filled the water cooler with colored gelatin), the prank war brought our team closer together. Laughter echoed through the hallways, breaking down barriers and creating bonds that transcended job titles and departments.

As the office move drew to a close, a ceasefire was declared—not because anyone ran out of ideas or enthusiasm, but because everyone realised that the true victory lay not in who pulled the most elaborate prank, but in the joy and camaraderie we had shared. The office returned to its usual rhythm in new surroundings, but the memories of the prank war lingered on as a reminder of the power of laughter and teamwork.

The legendary office move prank war taught us valuable lessons about creativity, collaboration, and the importance of levity in the workplace. It showed us that amidst deadlines and meetings, a shared laugh can be just as valuable as any strategic plan. Most importantly, it reinforced the bonds of friendship and camaraderie that make our office not just a place of work, but a community.

As we looked back on the prank war, we did so with fondness and gratitude for the memories created and the relationships strengthened. And who knows? Perhaps one day, when the time is right, the office will once again echo with the sound of laughter and the faint rustle of sticky notes—a reminder that in every workplace, a little mischief can go a long way.

What a Mug

Susan was predisposed to a good prank. I understand when she left the organisation a few months after me she removed all the communal mugs from the kitchen and replaced them with her own, bearing the smiling faces of herself and me. Apparently, this went down like a bucket of sick with the Trustees and the new CEO but personally I found it bloody hilarious. Nice one Susan.

Open Plan Problems: The Saga of the Communal Fridge

In the bustling hive of the office, where collaboration and camaraderie thrived, there existed a microcosm of shared joys and, inevitably, shared frustrations—the communal fridge. What began as a convenient spot to store lunches and snacks soon evolved into a saga of epic proportions, fraught with tales of mystery, mishaps, and the occasional culinary catastrophe.

Like many office fridges, ours started with the best of intentions—a place for employees to store their meals and beverages, ensuring they remained fresh until lunchtime. People labeled their food with colorful sticky notes, sharing friendly reminders to "Please do not eat!" or "Reserved for John's birthday party!"

As the office grew and the fridge filled to capacity, tensions began to simmer. Leftovers lingered longer than anticipated, transforming from tempting treats into science experiments. Occasionally, someone would mistake a colleague's carefully curated lunch for communal property, leading to passive-aggressive notes and muttered grievances.

Then came the day when the fridge went rogue. A malfunction left its contents perilously warm, turning perfectly edible meals into potential health hazards. Murmurs of discontent spread through the office like wildfire, prompting emergency meetings and impromptu cleaning sessions.

In an attempt to restore order, the office manager instituted a "Fridge Cleanup Day," complete with warnings of impending purges and stern reminders to label all items with names and dates. Yet, despite these efforts, the communal fridge remained a source of mild exasperation and occasional horror stories.

Stories emerged—of sandwiches gone missing, yogurt cups left to ferment, and the legendary jar of pickles that mysteriously vanished, only to reappear weeks later in a forgotten corner. The fridge became a topic of water cooler & hot tap gossip, its quirks and caprices woven into the fabric of office lore.

Despite its challenges, the communal fridge also provided moments of levity amidst the chaos. Office parties were planned around its contents, with impromptu potlucks celebrating birthdays and milestones. Colleagues bonded over shared frustrations, turning what could have been a sore spot into a quirky badge of office life.

As our office continued to navigate the saga of the communal fridge, we learned valuable lessons in communication, respect for shared spaces, and the importance of a well-maintained appliance. While the fridge may have occasionally tested our patience, it also serves as a reminder of the diverse personalities and daily routines that make our workplaces unique.

In the end, the communal fridge is more than just a storage unit for food—it's a reflection of our collective experiences, shared joys, and occasional mishaps. And as we navigate its challenges together, we do so with a sense of humor and camaraderie that defines our office culture—a culture where even the quirkiest of appliances can become a cherished part of our shared story.

Chapter 7:
Social Media Shenanigans

The Tweet That Went Viral for All the Wrong Reasons
In the fast-paced world of social media, where every post has the potential to reach thousands—or even millions—of eyes, a well-crafted tweet can elevate your organisation's profile or, as we discovered, lead to unforeseen consequences. This is the story of the tweet that went viral for all the wrong reasons, teaching us valuable lessons in communication, crisis management, and the power of digital influence.

It all started with good intentions. Our social media team Phillipa, eager to engage our online community and promote an upcoming fundraising event, crafted what they believed to be a witty and attention-grabbing tweet. The message highlighted the event's theme of community unity and invited followers to join us in making a difference.

However, within minutes of posting, the tweet sparked unexpected backlash. Critics accused us of cultural insensitivity, pointing out language and imagery in the tweet that inadvertently perpetuated harmful stereotypes. Comments flooded in, both from supporters confused by the negative reaction and detractors demanding an immediate apology.

Realising the gravity of the situation, our communications team, George swiftly went into damage control mode. We deleted the tweet and issued a public apology, acknowledging the hurt caused and reaffirming our commitment to inclusivity and sensitivity in all communications. However, the damage was done, and the tweet had already made its rounds across social media platforms.

In the aftermath, we conducted a thorough review of our social media policies and procedures. We implemented stricter approval processes for posts and invested in diversity training for our entire team to ensure cultural sensitivity in our messaging. We also engaged directly with community leaders and stakeholders to rebuild trust and learn from their perspectives.

While the experience was undoubtedly challenging, it also provided an opportunity for introspection and growth. We used the incident as a catalyst to strengthen our commitment to diversity, equity, and inclusion within our organisation. Our subsequent social media campaigns focused on celebrating diverse voices and uplifting marginalised communities, fostering meaningful engagement and positive change.

The tweet that went viral for all the wrong reasons taught us invaluable lessons about the power and pitfalls of social media. It reinforced the importance of thoughtful communication, genuine empathy, and proactive engagement with our community. As we continue our journey, we remain committed to using social media as a force for good, amplifying our mission while staying true to our values of respect and inclusivity.

In the fast-paced world of digital communication, every tweet carries weight. The tweet that once caused turmoil now serves as a reminder of our responsibility and opportunity to make a positive impact, one post at a time.

Meme Magic: Using Humor to Boost Donations

In the realm of nonprofit fundraising, creativity and innovation are key to capturing the attention—and hearts— of potential donors. This is the story of how we discovered the power of meme magic, harnessing humor to not only engage our audience but also inspire generosity in support of our cause.

It all began with a brainstorming session where our social media team sought new ways to connect with our online community. We recognised the widespread popularity of memes—humorous images and videos that spread rapidly across social media platforms—and wondered if we could leverage this cultural phenomenon to promote our fundraising efforts.

Armed with creativity and a keen understanding of our audience's interests, we set out to create memes that would resonate. We focused on weaving our charity's mission and message into relatable and humorous content. Whether it was a clever twist on a popular meme format, or a witty caption paired with a poignant image, each meme was designed to catch attention and spark conversation.

As we unleashed our memes on social media, the response was immediate and overwhelmingly positive. Followers eagerly shared our posts, tagging friends and family members, thus expanding our reach far beyond our usual audience. Memes became a conversation starter, drawing attention to our cause in a lighthearted and approachable manner.

With increased engagement came a surge in donations. Supporters who discovered us through memes expressed appreciation for our creative approach and were inspired to contribute to our cause. The memes not only raised awareness but also fostered a sense of community among donors, united by their shared appreciation for humor and their commitment to making a difference.

Encouraged by our success, we continued to innovate with memes, adapting our content to coincide with holidays, awareness months, and trending topics. Each meme served as a digital ambassador, inviting new supporters to learn about our mission and join our efforts in meaningful ways.

Meme magic became more than just a strategy—it became a core element of our digital fundraising playbook. We embraced the dynamic nature of social media, constantly iterating and refining our approach to keep our audience engaged and inspired.

Today, memes continue to play a pivotal role in outreach efforts, evolving alongside digital trends and societal shifts. They remind us that humor can be a powerful catalyst for change, breaking down barriers and fostering connections that transcend geography and demographics.

As we navigate the ever-changing landscape of nonprofit fundraising, we hold onto the belief that laughter is not just good medicine—it's also a potent tool for building a brighter future, one meme at a time.

Chapter 8:
International Incidents

Lost in Translation: When Our Slogan Meant Something Entirely Different Overseas

In the globalised world of nonprofit work, expanding our reach beyond borders brings both opportunities and unforeseen challenges. This is the tale of a well-intentioned slogan that took on a life of its own in a foreign land, teaching us valuable lessons in cultural sensitivity and the importance of local context.

It all started during a brainstorming session aimed at refreshing our charity's public image. We wanted a slogan that encapsulated our mission of empowerment and community support. After careful deliberation, we settled on a phrase that resonated deeply with our team and supporters alike.

With enthusiasm and optimism, we unveiled our new slogan across our website, social media channels, and marketing materials. The response from our local community was overwhelmingly positive, reaffirming our belief that we had struck the right chord with our messaging.

Buoyed by our success at home, we embarked on an ambitious international campaign to raise awareness. Our slogan, translated meticulously by professional linguists, was rolled out in multiple languages, promising to resonate universally with audiences around the world.

However, our excitement soon turned to consternation when reports surfaced from one of our international contacts. It appeared that our slogan, when translated into the local language, carried unintended connotations that were not aligned with our charitable mission. Instead of inspiring support, it elicited confusion and even amusement among the local population.

Swiftly recognising the cultural misstep, we took immediate action to address the situation. We issued a public apology, explaining our oversight and reaffirming our commitment to respectful and culturally sensitive communication. Moreover, we engaged local advisors and community leaders to revise the slogan in a way that authentically reflected our mission while resonating positively with the local audience.

The experience served as a poignant reminder of the complexities of cross-cultural communication. We implemented rigorous review processes for all international communications, ensuring that translations undergo thorough scrutiny by native speakers and cultural experts. Additionally, we embraced a more collaborative approach with our international partners, valuing their insights and perspectives in crafting messages that resonate authentically across diverse cultural landscapes.

While the journey was marked by initial missteps, it ultimately strengthened our resolve to bridge cultures and build meaningful connections worldwide. Our renewed commitment to cultural sensitivity and inclusive communication continues to guide our efforts as we strive to make a positive impact, one community at a time.

The saga of our lost-in-translation slogan serves as a testament to the transformative power of humility, empathy, and a willingness to learn from our mistakes. In the tapestry of our international work, it remains a thread that reminds us of the importance of respecting and celebrating the rich diversity of our global community.

The lost in translation works both ways of course. I must admit I was a little amused when a young intern from the US insisted on wearing his lapel badge – Stand Up to Trump! I say no more.

Less enlightened was being picked up by colleagues in Prague to be taken to conference with a van having the "Handicapped People" blazened along the side. Apparently, this is quite acceptable speech in the Czech Republic.

The Day I Learned What "Business Casual" Means in Different Countries

In the interconnected world of global business, navigating cultural nuances is essential for effective communication and professional etiquette. This is the story of my enlightening journey into understanding the varied interpretations of "business casual" across different countries, and the humorous (yet insightful) lessons learned along the way.

Armed with what I thought was a clear understanding of "business casual"—a blend of professional attire with a relaxed, less formal touch—I embarked on a series of international meetings and conferences, confident in my sartorial choices.

My first lesson was with Japanese colleagues, where I quickly discovered that "business casual" meant impeccably tailored suits, even in summer heat. My attempt at an open neck shirt and khakis garnered polite but bemused looks, hinting that I had missed the mark.

In France, "business casual" embraced a more fashionable flair, with a preference for chic blazers and designer loafers. Casual Fridays still upheld a certain elegance that contrasted sharply with the relaxed attire I associated with the term.

Crossing the Atlantic to the United States, I encountered a more relaxed interpretation of "business casual." Here, chenos and button-down shirts were acceptable, and casual Fridays often saw jeans and trainers making their appearance in corporate settings—a stark departure from the formalities observed in Asia and Europe.

In Bermuda, shorts, long socks blazer & no tie.

Each new revelation prompted me to adapt my wardrobe and mindset, accordingly, seeking to align with local expectations while respecting cultural norms. It was a lesson in flexibility and cultural empathy, understanding that perceptions of professional attire varied widely and were deeply rooted in local customs and corporate cultures.

Ultimately, my journey into the world of "business casual" underscored the richness of global diversity and the importance of sensitivity to cultural differences. It encouraged me to approach every international interaction with an open mind and a willingness to learn, embracing the opportunity to bridge cultural divides through respectful engagement.

Armed with newfound insights, I continue to navigate the complexities of international business with a blend of professionalism and cultural awareness. Each encounter serves as a reminder of the transformative power of understanding and embracing diversity, both in attire and in the broader spectrum of human interactions.

The day I learned what "business casual" means in different countries was not just about clothing—it was a journey of enlightenment, fostering deeper connections and appreciation for the diverse tapestry of global business etiquette.

My favourite, Bermuda by far.

Chapter 9:
The Lighter Side of Legalities

Navigating the Labyrinth of Charity Law with a Sense of Humour

In the complex world of nonprofit management, understanding and adhering to charity law can feel like navigating a labyrinth. With regulations and compliance issues at every turn, maintaining a sense of humor is essential to staying sane. This chapter recounts some of the more memorable moments in our legal journey, where laughter proved to be the best tool for navigating the intricacies of charity law.

The Paperwork Avalanche

Starting a charity involves a mountain of paperwork—articles of incorporation, bylaws, tax-exempt status applications, and more. My first encounter with this avalanche was daunting, to say the least. Amidst the stacks of forms and legal jargon, we decided to lighten the mood with a filing party, complete with snacks and a "Most Forms Filled Without Crying" award. It didn't make the paperwork any less, but it certainly made the process more bearable.

Board Meeting Bingo

Board meetings are essential for governance, but they can sometimes be long and, dare I say, tedious. Sitting through these meetings knowing you will never get that part of your life back. To keep spirits high, the senior management team (SMT) turned to Board Meeting Bingo. Each SMT member received a bingo card with phrases like "fiduciary responsibility," "budget amendment," "strategic plan." etc. The first to get a bingo as a result of Trustees reverting to these phrases won a prize—usually something humorous. It kept everyone engaged and brought a much-needed dose of laughter to the proceedings.

The Oops Clause.
Every charity's bylaws need a catch-all clause for unforeseen circumstances. I dubbed ours the "Oops Clause," a lighthearted nod to the inevitable mistakes and oversights that come with running a nonprofit. Whenever someone mentioned the "Oops Clause" in a meeting, it was a reminder to take ourselves a little less seriously and embrace the learning curve.

The Audit Antics
Annual audits are a necessary but nerve-wracking part of nonprofit life. To ease the tension, we turned our audit preparation into a game show called "Audit Antics." Staff members were contestants, and the audit committee played the role of the stern judges. We answered questions, performed mock interviews, and even had a lightning round on compliance trivia. By the time the real auditors arrived, we were well-prepared and far less stressed.

However, one young auditor arrived at our offices, very proper and clearly quite new in the role. He went through the books and on a number of occasions asked exactly how many people the charity employed. Clearly not satisfied with the same answer he asked very loudly and a very accusational tone; "Well the who is Henry, I keep overhearing his name in conversations?"

"Henry, that's the hoover." I said in a very straight face much to the embarrassment of the young auditor who had thought there was something more untoward afoot.

Trademark Tremors
Protecting our charity's brand involved navigating the intricate world of trademarks. Our initial application was

returned with a request for clarification on our logo's "distinctiveness." In an attempt to illustrate our point, we submitted a series of increasingly absurd logo designs, from a dancing dog to a solemn-looking hound. The exercise not only helped clarify our actual logo's uniqueness but also provided much-needed comic relief. Sadly, our *Purple Hound* was never born.

While the labyrinth of charity law is complex and sometimes daunting, approaching it with a sense of humor has made all the difference. Our journey through the legal landscape has been filled with unexpected twists and turns, but laughter has been our constant companion. It reminds us that even in the most serious of endeavors, there's always room for a little levity.

By infusing humor into our legal processes, we've not only stayed sane but also fostered a positive and collaborative environment. In the end, the lighter side of legalities has taught us that the best way to navigate the labyrinth is with a smile, a laugh, and the occasional rubber chicken.

Chapter 10:
Because Even CEO's need a Holiday

The cut and thrust of the role of a CEO means inevitably the need to wind down and take a break, but sadly even this down time can go wrong.

The Trip of a Lifetime

It was my other half's 50th birthday so we wanted it to be a bit special, accordingly we went to Kenya for a trip of a lifetime – a Safari! And what trip it was.

Baboons love Socks!

We had been warned that the baboons were quite noisy and given the opportunity would try and sneak into the chalet and steal whatever they could lay their hands on, but particularly socks?

Now clearly, I did not fully believe all of this and true to form we managed to leave an entry point to our room. We came back from lunch to find a baboon sitting at the end of the bed, rifling through my socks – I kid you not. I did the obvious thing, made myself look as big and fearsome as possible and chased him out. Well, when I say chased, he sort of sauntered out in his own time. I gave the roar of a winner as he left, and he turned round and roared back bearing the biggest teeth I have ever been close too. I am so glad that it did not turn into a full fist fight as I might have lost my whole wardrobe.

Colonel Saito Arrives

Later the same day as Babbongate, there was a bit of a kerfuffle outside the room and looked out to see a large group of Chinese tourists had arrived under the strict control of their group director who complete with Safari jacket, pith hat and cane under his arm, was the spitting image of the Japanese Colonel Saito from the 1957 classic – *The Bridge over the River Kwai*. He proceeded to "direct" & shout at his charges in the same manner and they all scurried off to do whatever he had instructed.

Hippos' - Cute & Cuddly – they are not

Later that evening, after dinner there was again a bit of a commotion outside the chalet. I went to go out, just to be nosey really but before I did, I thought I would open the curtains. I was very glad I made that decision as the commotion in fact was caused by a herd of hippopotamuses wandering through the camp.

Lucky for us, I closed the curtains as quickly as I opened them protected only by a thin pane of glass. While hippos don't typically hunt humans as prey, they can be very aggressive and according to the BBC kill about 500 people each year.

Never Smile at a Crocodile

I admit I have an irrational fear of crocodiles, not usually a day-to-day problem in Hampshire where we live but Africa raises this fear to a whole new level.

Walking from our very nice safari hut to the restaurant along a properly made-up path I spotted in the distance a statue of a huge crocodile lying about 15 feet from the path. I smiled hesitantly as we passed as I even have issues with blow up Lie-low crocodiles. On getting to the restaurant our guides asked if we saw the croc? Apparently, he is very real and turns up daily for feeding from the restaurant staff! The other useful tip they gave was "Check the pool before getting in, as he often goes for a dip himself."

The next day the croc was not there, I think that scared me more.

My Very First Hostage Situation

Travelling further into the bush we were part of a two-jeep convoy. We had been travelling for hours, or so it felt travelling on the dodgy roads. Up ahead some boulders were across the road so our driver, John slowed down. As we did so 30 or so local tribesmen appeared from nowhere placing boulders behind the jeeps. We could not go forward nor back due to the rocks. To our left was thick bush and to our right a steep V shaped ravine. We were stuck.

John and the other driver got out and spoke to the Elders. It would seem there had been goat rustling the night before, it had all got rather nasty, and the Elders wanted the local authorities to take some action. They felt detaining us might produce that action from the authorities. It was all quite reasonable at first and we took it in our stride expecting a delay of an hour or so while the local police turned up.

After a couple of hours news came back that the police would not be coming. It was at that point that machetes and other unpleasant looking weapons appeared, again from nowhere.

John and the other driver looked at each other and, in an instant, jumped in the jeeps, started the engines and said hang on. They cut down into the ravine travelling at an angle of 45 degrees at about 50 mph. All sorts of shouting and objects were thrown but the tribesmen were taken off guard and we got through, looking like something out of an SAS movie.

The jeeps were badly dented, and the other jeep had a smashed windscreen, but everyone was safe & sound. Best driving I have ever experienced, but a strong case for new underware all round.

Hurricane Irma

Let's go to Cuba I said, it will be fun and I have found a deal! We booked, we went but it was only on arrival did I realise I had got a good deal because it was Hurrican Season. "It will be fine, what could possibly go wrong." Well a Category 5, Hurricane Irma was the answer to that.

We saw on the TV that Hurricane Irma was picking up a bit of strength and heading towards Cuba. The hotel made preparations, cutting down old palm tree leaves, boarding up windows etc but it was only when we heard that the local dolphins had been air lifted out that it might be a bit of an issue. We would have to stay and sit it out.

The hotel staff told us to meet in the restaurant for instructions, which we did. They were worried about the storm surge so asked us to stay in the restaurant which was some 3-4m above ground level. Sadly, though they expected a surge height of about 5m. Now I have never sailed anything around a dining room before but will give it a go and located a suitable bit of furniture which I thought would meet our needs. The surge danger came and went without trouble, but the wind started picking up.

Soon the roof started to lift and then disappear. We were moved to smaller and smaller rooms as the wind grew and bits of the hotel flew away. We sat through it hot, sticky, hungry and to be honest with a little bit of concern but the

Dunkirk Spirit kicked in and everyone shared what they had and chatted as if nothing was really happening.

Eventually, the storm gone, we were led back to our rooms in small groups. It looked like something out of the *Poseidon Adventure* with bits of building gone or badly damaged, electrical cables buzzing dangerously close to water and barly passable walkways.

We got back to our rooms which were untouched. In hindsight we would have been safer and more comfortable sitting it out in our rooms but the Cubans did all they could to make us safe.

The next day we had a look round at the devastation. Buildings badly damaged, debris everywhere and every stick of the beach bar completely gone. Hotel staff & guests alike mucked in and soon the hotel was looking in a much better state.

The Chefs, having lost power to their fridges & freezers decided the best way forward was to BBQ everything. This turned into a great "After Party" and frankly the BBQ I have ever attended. To be honest the only real impact on us was there no ice for the G & Ts! We were air lifted out two days later.

Hurricane Irma hit Cuba in September 2017, It was the first Category 5 hurricane to hit Cuba in nearly a century, directly causing ten deaths, damaging tens of thousands of homes and destroying hundreds of poultry farms. The capital Havana suffered the effect of 27 ft waves and dreadful flooding.

DeJja Vue – Hurricane Beryl

Lightning doesn't strikethe same place twice - correct? Well maybe it does. Not wanting to be caught in another hurricane we decided to visit Mexico in June/July well ahead of the hurricane season.

Hurricane Beryl approached the Yucatan peninsula in Mexico in late June 2024, one of the earliest hurricanes on record. This time we were prepared and knew what to expect. Again, the hotel staff made preparations, but we were advised to stay in our rooms – we got in the essential supplies (ie Vodka, Tequila) and sat it out. Compared to Irma this was but a breeze, but still removing some roofs off of thatched buildings and downing old palm trees etc.

My concern here was not the winds but the surge tide which I thought might encourage the local freshwater crocodiles to come a-paddling up the walkways. Again, irrational fear maybe, but I thought I had good reason to be concerned. Worse than that though, there was a chap whose job was on the beach to blow a whistle to get people out of the water if the saltwater crocs got too close. Have you seen the size of those things? I would have been happier if he had a shotgun as well as a bloody whistle.

Fortunately, there was no real damage at our hotel and again the Mexican staff did everything they could to keep us safe. I was concerned though about the vulture looking birds circling overhead. What did they know I didnt? The good news was that the power being maintained there was ice for the G & Ts.

Hurricane Beryl was a rare early season major hurricane in June 2024 when it reached Category 4 status.

It hit Mexico as a Category 2 hurricane but still caused millions of dollars' worth of damage and taking 10 lives.

Another Great Escape

It all started with what was supposed to be a relaxing holiday in the Dominican Republic with Maggie and our good friends Dot & Rod. We had planned this trip for months envisioning endless days of sunbathing, tropical cocktails, and maybe a little salsa dancing. What we didn't plan for was Dot being held hostage in a hospital scam.

It all began innocently enough. Dot decided to try a curry at the hotel before we left for the Dominican Republic. All well & good but on day two, her stomach rebelled. After a particularly dramatic episode in the hotel bathroom, Rod insisted Dot go to the hotel doctor who very quickly directed them to a local hospital, not the nearest hospital as it transpired.

The hospital looked legitimate enough – white walls, people in scrubs, that distinct antiseptic smell. A nurse with a smile that was just a little too wide for comfort immediately ushered Dot into a room and hooked her up to an IV drip. Rod waited, flipping through outdated magazines and wondering if "salsa dancing" had been a euphemism for "writhing in pain." Confirmation from the UK was received that their holiday insurance would cover any costs, BUT this particular hospital was "known to the insurance company" and might be a scam.

Two days passed, and Dot didn't come out. Rod approached the nurse, whose smile had now become eerily unsettling, and asked about his wife. "She's very sick," she said, her voice dripping with faux concern. "She needs to stay here and receive treatment. But don't worry, we'll take good care of her. It will only cost $5,000."

Rod's heart sank. This was no hospital. This was a scam! He needed to get Dot out of there before they drained both his wallet and his will to live, let alone pump more unnecessary drugs into Dot.

That night, we devised a plan. Maggie, a nurse of many years standing & armed with essential items from a travel First Aid kit entered the hospital. Rod phoned through to the Nurses station to say Dot was discharging herself. "No, not possible" was the immediate response, but on insisting it was agreed Dot could go, once someone had removed the drip which might take another 24 hours or so!

With that the escape plan shifted into gear. Rod & I went to reception to complete the paperwork while Maggie removed Dot from the drip and then joined us. While Rod completed the biggest pile of paperwork you can imagine, I sorted a taxi and kept the security guard engaged in light conversation. He had good English, so we spoke about the need for a security guard in a hospital and the need for a guard to carry a Glock 17 9mm Luger pistol in A&E. The irony did not escape me.

The taxi arrived & we rushed out the door, past a confused receptionist &my new found friend the security guard, and into the taxi making good our escape. On examining the paperwork, the hospital had added an extra day to Dot's stay as they *work on Madrid time rather than local time*? The insurance company paid the bills and Dot made a full recovery, eventually. Just another holiday story when travelling with the Hills.

Our daughters now want the right to veto any holiday destinations we might suggest, and our friends check where we are going so, they can avoid the same part of the world. Bognor beckons for next year!

Chapter 11: Reflections

Amidst the chaos of charity work, there have been countless heartwarming moments that reminded me why we do what we do. Here are a few that stand out.

The Joy of Giving

Seeing the joy on a non verbal child's face when they get to experience a high speed boat ride, or a family's relief when they find a safe place to stay—these moments are priceless and fuel our passion to continue.

Stories of Transformation

Witnessing individuals transform their lives through our programs is incredibly rewarding. From overcoming addiction to finding stable employment, these success stories are a testament to the impact of our work.

Community Spirit

The sense of community and solidarity at our events, where people from all walks of life come together for a common cause, is truly inspiring. It's a reminder that when we unite, we can achieve incredible things.

Chapter 12:
The Wisdom of the Firm Handshake

Lessons Learned from a Lifetime in Charity

Throughout my career in the charity sector, one constant has been the firm handshake—a symbol of trust, respect, and commitment. Each handshake has come with its own set of lessons, shaping my approach to leadership, relationships, and making a difference in the world. Here are some of the most valuable lessons learned from a lifetime in charity.

The Power of Presence

A firm handshake demands presence. It's about being fully in the moment, acknowledging the person in front of you. In charity work, being present means truly listening to the needs and stories of those we aim to help, ensuring that our efforts are both impactful and empathetic.

Building Trust

Trust is the cornerstone of any relationship, and a handshake often sets the tone. Whether it's with donors, volunteers, or beneficiaries, building trust is crucial. It's about keeping promises, being transparent, and consistently acting with integrity.

Embracing Change

Working in the Third Sector is dynamic, with constant changes and challenges. A firm handshake signifies readiness to face these head-on. Embracing change with resilience and adaptability has been essential in navigating the evolving landscape of nonprofit work.

Leadership and Accountability

Leading a charity involves making tough decisions and being accountable for them. A firm handshake is a commitment to leadership, signaling that we stand by our actions and decisions, ready to take responsibility and learn from our experiences.

Chapter 13:
Future Plans

From Firm Handshakes to Even Firmer Hugs

As I look to the future, my commitment to making a difference remains unwavering albeit now in a voluntary role. As the Chair of a Disability organisation on the south coast I plan to expand our programs, reach more communities, and deepen our impact. And while a firm handshake will always be a symbol of our commitment, I am also embracing the warmth and compassion of even firmer hugs, signifying our dedication to building a more inclusive and supportive world.

A good handshake transcends professional boundaries—it's a gesture that builds connections, fosters trust, and shows respect in every aspect of life. Whether in work, community, or personal relationships, the principles behind a firm handshake—presence, trust, and respect—are universally valuable.

A Guide to Perfecting Your Own Signature Handshake

1. **Be Present**: Make eye contact and focus on the person in front of you.

2. **Be Confident**: A firm grip (but not too strong) conveys confidence.

3. **Be Respectful**: Shake hands with a genuine smile and show respect.

4. **Be Authentic**: Let your handshake reflect your true self.

Final Thoughts: Embracing the Unexpected with a Smile

In the journey of charity work, and in life, embracing the unexpected with a smile and a sense of humour has been my guiding principle. Challenges are inevitable, but with resilience, humour, and a firm handshake, we can navigate them successfully. Here's to the countless handshakes—and hugs—yet to come, and to the incredible impact we can make together.

About the Author

Ted Hill was born and raised in St Albans in Hertfordshire marrying Maggie in 1980. They have three daughters and seven grandchildren. Starting life working in research chemistry at ICI, Ted changed his career to the Third Sector spending over 40 years working at a senior level, mostly as CEO of local, regional and national charities.

Ted holds an LLB(Hons) law degree and a Masters in Organisational Development from Middlesex University. He is a Fellow of the Royal Society of Public Health (FRSPH) and until his retirement was a Fellow of the Institute of Leadership & Management (FInstLM).

His own volunteering was with Sea Cadets where he was the Hertfordshire District Officer (SCC - RNR) before moving to Hamble Le Rice on the south coast of England in 2018.

Ted was awarded an MBE for his work in the Third Sector in 2012. He retired in 2022 and now volunteers as boat crew and fundraiser for Wetwheels Hamble for which he is also Chair.